Contents

CREDITS: *Joni Prittie: Designer, Artist. Irene Morris: Graphic Design. Todd Tsukushi: Photography. Location: Kelly Heim Interiors, Los Altos, CA. Special Thanks to Cynthia, Mike, Family and Friends, and to Dutch Run Designs, Soquel, California, for their wonderful Father Christmas Carving.* © 1991, Joni Prittie

CHRISTMAS CANDLELIGHT

Perfect roses entwined in pine and glistening gold ribbons capture the candlelight of special holiday entertaining. Display this soft wreath of roses and light in the entry hall or as the centerpiece for Christmas dinner. The secret of how simple to create this lovely candle ring will be yours to keep...

MATERIALS

7 large cream silk roses

5 cream silk rosebuds

1 18 inch oval wreath of artificial pine

36 dark red berries, wired in groups of three

1 1/2 yard 1 1/2 inch wire edge gold ribbon

1 bunch gold, glittered gypsophila (Baby's Breath)

Glue gun/glue sticks

1 large round candle for ring center, white, green or red

Optional materials for waxing roses:

2 cream colored candles

5 drops rose oil

Double boiler

 1 If roses are to be waxed, follow instructions in oval.

 **2** Cut rose stems to three inches and glue roses and bud wires into pine wreath. Space roses evenly.

 3 Glue berries and gypsophila to wreath among roses. Gypsophila (Baby's Breath) can be sprayed with gold glitter while paint is wet.

 4 Tie a large four loop bow with streamers and secure bow to wreath as pictured.

 5 Place round candle in center of ring. As candle burns down, replace with another tall candle. Flames should never come close to dried or artificial materials.

Cream silk roses have been dipped in melted wax to create a gossamer effect. Simply melt white or cream wax or candles in a double boiler. Add rose oil to the melted wax to scent. Hold individual roses by wire and dip flower head into liquid. Place waxed flower stems in an oasis block until wax hardens, usually just a few minutes.

HOLIDAY PILLOWS

Holiday accent pillows set the mood so beautifully. It is always the small touches that complete the feelings in a special setting...

MATERIALS FOR PILLOW A

1 7 inch square green velvet pillow

26 inches small red cording

4 small red tassels

1 cream linen heart shape—trace heart pattern on page 44

14 inches red ribbon rose trim

1 small red rose heart applique

24 inches 1/4 inch cream ribbon

Glue gun/glue sticks

1 Trace heart pattern on page 44. Cut one heart of cream linen. Glue heart to pillow center.

2 Glue ribbon rose trim around heart. Tie small four loop bow of cream ribbon. Glue bow to heart center and glue applique to bow center.

3 Glue red cording around pillow edge and glue one red tassel to each pillow corner.

MATERIALS FOR CHRISTMAS TREE PILLOW

1 7 inch square red velvet pillow piped in green velvet

1 4 inch square cream linen

1 green cotton Christmas tree shape

18 inches 3/8 inch gold ribbon with green edging

12 inches 3/8 inch green, red and gold striped ribbon

1 red ribbon rose

1 inch 3/8 inch red ribbon

21 small gold beads

Fabric glue

Glue gun/glue sticks

1 Glue cream linen square to pillow center.

Pattern

2 Glue tree shape to center of square using fabric glue. Glue 1 inch piece red ribbon to tree bottom. Glue ribbon rose center of red ribbon.

3 Glue gold beads to tree. Glue gold ribbon around square, making sure to square off corners. If ribbon will not fold and glue evenly, simply cut ribbon as shown and glue in place. Tie a small bow of striped ribbon and glue to lower left corner of center bow.

DECORATOR SHADES

Cranberry red, cream and deep Christmas green printed cotton is simply fused or glued to a plain lampshade for a little holiday flavor. Our shade can be used throughout the year or saved for display at Christmas.

MATERIALS

1 7 inch deep lampshade—soft green

1/4 yard red, green and cream floral chintz

2 1/2 yards 1/4 inch cranberry cording

Fabric glue or 1/4 yard fusible sheet

Glue gun/glue sticks

1 Following instructions on fusible sheets or fabric glue, prepare shapes cut from printed fabric.

2 Glue or fuse shape to lampshade, allowing design to flow around entire shade.

3 Glue cord to both top and bottom of shade 1/2 inch from edges.

White or cream lampshades can be painted quite easily. Acrylic craft paints work very well; or use paint with an almost equal amount of water. Lightly moisten entire shade with warm water before painting. Apply warm water with a sponge and paint with a flat brush or sponge. Use quick, even strokes to avoid streaking.

Easy Picture Bows

Presents all tied in bows of silk and lace...why not add Victorian picture bows to prints and paintings for the holidays. Moire and silks are perfect bow fabrics. Make picture bows for each season of the year.

MATERIALS FOR FRENCH MEDALLION BOW

1/4 yard scarlet moire fabric

1 5 inch square light cardboard

Glue gun/glue sticks

1 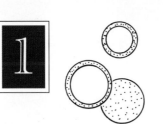 Cut one 2 1/2 inch circle of cardboard. Set aside. Using these circles as patterns, placed on wrong-side of moire fabric, draw pattern and allow 1/4 inch "seam" allowance. Use larger cardboard circle pattern to cut two 3 inch circles of moire.

2  Glue 1 1/2 inch circle of moire to 1 inch cardboard circle as shown. This will create the button used for medallion center.

3  Glue one of remaining moire circles to 2 1/2 inch cardboard circle to create medallion base. Fabric edges will be gathered to back side of cardboard. Set remaining moire circle aside.

4  Cut eight 4 1/2 inch by 2 1/2 inch strips of moire fabric. Fold and glue each strip as shown.

5  Assemble medallion as shown, gluing each loop in place and adding button as final step.

6  Cut one 6 inch by 8 inch strip of moire ribbon and glue as shown. Gather and glue top edge to back of center medallion. Iron a small turned edge on remaining moire circle and carefully glue this circle to medallion back for a finished effect.

VICTORIAN DESK SET

Christmas notes and cards sent and received with such love...time to sit quietly at the writing desk, reflecting on the year almost past.

COVERED BOOK MATERIALS

1 Address book, notebook or diary

1/4 yard green velvet

1 yard 1/4 inch deep green ribbon

1 gold filigree metal earring finding

1 jeweled ruby

8 smaller jewels—emeralds, rhinestones or gold beads

Fabric marking pen

Glue gun/glue sticks

PENCIL HOLDER MATERIALS

1 cardboard pencil holder or other small can

1 5 inch by 10 inch piece green velvet

20 inches 3/8 inch gold braid

1 gold filigree metal earring finding

1 1 inch jeweled ruby

18 to 20 small gold beads

Fabric glue

Glue gun/glue sticks

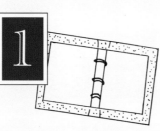

1 Place book on wrong-side of fabric and mark fabric as shown, allowing approximately one inch allowance for gluing. Cut fabric along marked lines.

4 Glue velvet around cylinder. Use fabric glue to secure velvet to inside of pencil holder.

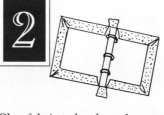

2 Glue fabric to book as shown, beginning with back cover. Notch fabric at top and bottom of book spine. After front and back cover are secured with glue, simply push these fabric tabs into place.

5 Glue braid around top of holder, 1/2 inch from top edge. Glue braid to inside of pencil holder on top of velvet edge for a finished look.

3 Glue ribbon to inside cover, over fabric edges to create a finished look. Glue gold filigree and jewels in place on book.

6 Glue filigree and stones in place on front of pencil holder.

LETTER OPENER

Cover letter opener by laying opener on white paper and drawing around handle shape. Cut paper to make a pattern, then use pattern to cut two pieces of green velvet. Glue velvet shapes to front and back of handle. Glue 3/8 inch gold cording around handle edges and bottom. Glue small jewels or trim to handle to complete.

Health, Peace, and sweet content be yours.
Shakespeare

ROSE AND PINE MANTLE GARLAND

Deck the halls with Christmas garlands. Armoires, doorways and mantles all hung with boughs of gathered pine and glorious silk ribbons, greet holiday visitors.

MATERIALS

1 50 inch raffia braid

10 large cream silk roses

9 cream silk rosebuds

20 stems artificial pine

1 bunch dried poppy seed pods

39 red berries wired in groups of three

1 bunch preserved gypsophila

7 to 10 green silk leaves

3 yards 1 1/2 inch gold and red patterned wire edge ribbon

Florist wire

Glue gun/glue sticks

 Working on a flat surface, glue pine to raffia braid.

 Glue roses and buds to braid, tucked in among pine. Glue green silk leaves to garland. Glue gypsophila sprigs to garland.

 Glue pods and berries to garland. Glue gypsophila sprigs to garland.

 Tie a large four loop bow with long streamers along garland length, securing with glue dots. Garlands can be hung in place by twisting loops of florist wire along garland length.

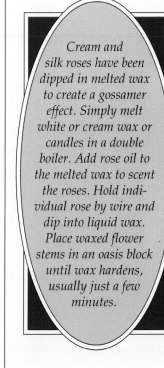

Cream and silk roses have been dipped in melted wax to create a gossamer effect. Simply melt white or cream wax or candles in a double boiler. Add rose oil to the melted wax to scent the roses. Hold individual rose by wire and dip into liquid wax. Place waxed flower stems in an oasis block until wax hardens, usually just a few minutes.

STOCKINGS FOR CHRISTMAS

As Christmas Eve approaches...stockings of lace and roses are hung. Wishes will soon be replaced with treasures...

MATERIALS

2 pieces beige brocade 12 inches by 15 inches

1 yard 1 inch lace trim with pearled center

18 inches 4 inch cream ruffled lace

18 inches cream ribbon rose trim

18 inches scalloped pearl trim

12 inches 3/8 inch cream lace

1 large cream silk ribbon rose

1 yard 3/4 inch cream brocade ribbon

8 inches 1/4 inch cream ribbon

Glue gun/glue sticks

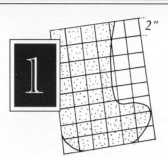

1 Cut two pieces of beige brocade to above measurements.

2 Fold a one inch top on each stocking shape and glue in place to wrong-side of fabric.

3 Glue stocking shapes together, taking care that glue is flattened along seam. Raw edges will be covered with lace trim.

4 Glue 3/8 inch lace trim to stocking, forming a toe and heel shape.

5 Glue pearl centered lace around edges of stocking shape.

6 Glue ruffled lace around stocking top. Glue scalloped pearl trim and ribbon rose trim to top portion of ruffle.

7 Tie a six loop bow and glue to upper left corner of stocking front. Glue large ribbon rose to bow center. Glue hanging loop to stocking, using 1/4 inch cream ribbon.

TURN OF THE CENTURY BELL PULL

December snow falls quietly... the sitting room inside is warm and glowing. Christmas tea is about to be served and shared with dear friends.

MATERIALS

1/4 yard cream moire fabric

1/4 yard fusible adhesive

1/4 yard cream cotton or other backing fabric

2 yards 1 inch gold braid or filigree trim

2 yards 3/8 inch forest green gross grain ribbon

1 yard 2 1/2 inch tapestry ribbon

12 inches gold cord

1 6 inch green silk tassel

1 7 inch bell pull dowel

Fabric glue

Glue gun/glue sticks

1 Following instructions on fusible adhesive information sheet, iron adhesive to wrong-side of a 6 inch by 30 inch strip of moire fabric.

2 Cut one 5 inch by 30 inch strip of backing fabric and iron to center back of moire as shown. Fold excess moire around edge of backing fabric and iron in place.

3 Fold bottom of strip and trim to shape. Bell pull can remain a rectangular shape if desired.

4 Glue tapestry ribbon down the center of moire strip, trimming the ribbon to follow shape of bell pull. Glue gross grain ribbon along tapestry ribbon edge for a finished look.

5 Glue gold trim along bell pull edges.

6 Glue top of bell pull around dowel and tie or glue gold cord to dowel ends to create a hanger. To complete, glue silk tassel to shaped end of bell pull.

YULETIDE PICTURE FRAME
&
NESTED CHRISTMAS BIRD

Family photographs bring those we love closer during the Christmas season. Happy gatherings filled with stories and laughter...Christmas time has arrived once again.

MATERIALS FOR YULETIDE PICTURE FRAME

1 small gold frame

3 sprigs cedar

3 sprigs dried German statice

7 small red berries

12 inches 3/4 inch green gross grain ribbon

Glue gun/glue sticks

MATERIALS FOR NESTED CHRISTMAS BIRD

1 small woven nest

1 small bird

Small amount dried green leaves

Few sprigs dried lavender

1 small stem pepper berries

5 inches 1/4 inch red ribbon

Glue gun/glue sticks

 Glue cedar, berries and German statice to top left hand corner of frame. Form a crescent shape to frame photograph.

 Tie a small four loop bow and glue to corner of frame. Shape ribbon streamers and attach with dots of glue.

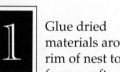 Glue dried materials around rim of nest to form a soft wreath effect and place small bird in her nest. Small nests can be filled with tiny gifts and hung on the tree.

POTPOURRI BASKET

Mossy baskets of spicy scents welcome all to a room filled with thoughts of Christmas. Gather and dry roses from the summer garden for decorating and freshening at Christmas time.

MATERIALS

1 8 inch moss covered basket

1 bunch dried German statice

12 dried roses or rosebuds

1 bunch artificial blackberries

1 bunch artificial cherries

6 small green silk leaves

1 yard each burgundy red and deep moss green ribbons

1 inch wire edged ribbon

Glue gun/glue sticks

1 Glue dried materials and berries around top edge of basket to form a wreath or small garland effect. Glue in green silk leaves near dried roses.

2 Use both ribbons together and tie a bow having six loops on each side. Three loops will be red, three will be green. Fluff bow and glue to top of basket handle. Drape ribbon streamers down each handle side.

Small baskets of all kinds can be easily covered with dried moss. Simply glue small amounts of moss to basket until entire surface is covered. Create wonderful scented baskets by gluing potpourri to basket.

DECEMBER

MERRIE XMAS

EXQUISITE COVERED BOXES

Tassels and rosebuds, lace and brocade easily decorate covered boxes. Gifts of chocolate, potpourri or imported soaps are gratefully received with such a perfect presentation.

MATERIALS FOR BOX B

1 heart shaped wooden box

1/4 yard wine moire fabric

1/8 yard light cotton batting

24 inches light green tassel trimmed gimp

48 inches small pearl trim

7 inches 1 inch pearl centered cream lace

8 small dried roses with leaves

12 inches 1/4 inch cranberry red ribbon

Fabric glue

Glue gun/glue sticks

1 Lay box top on reverse-side of fabric, draw around heart shape and cut two hearts—one to exact size and one heart with an approximate 1/2 inch margin around shape. Exact sized heart will cover bottom and larger heart will be used for top.

2 Cut one heart shape from cotton batting. This heart should be slightly smaller than box top. Glue batting shape to box top, using glue gun.

3 Using fabric glue, glue largest moire heart to box top, covering batting and securing fabric to top sides. Notch heart indentation for easy gluing.

4 Measure around bottom of box and cut one strip of moire to the correct dimensions. Remember to allow for top of box clearances when closing box. Glue strip to box sides. Glue remaining heart shape to bottom of box.

5 Use glue gun to glue tasseled gimp around sides of box top. Glue pearl trim to both top and bottom edges of gimp. To finish, glue lace strip diagonally across box top and glue roses and a small cranberry red bow in place.

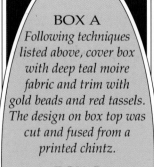

BOX A
Following techniques listed above, cover box with deep teal moire fabric and trim with gold beads and red tassels. The design on box top was cut and fused from a printed chintz.

BOX C
Cover a heart shaped box with soft green brocade and small dried yellow rosebuds. Rosebuds can usually be found in bulk at health food stores.

BOX A

BOX B

BOX C

CHRISTMAS TEA TOPIARY

Scones with butter and strawberry jam are all the more delicious served on a table dressed for Christmas tea.

MATERIALS FOR TOPIARY

1 double topiary form of Styrofoam™ and dowels

35 picks of artificial pine, sprigs separated

36 red berries, wired in groups of three

36 small dried roses and buds

3 stems artificial

Queen Anne's lace

3 stems dried white gypsophila

2 yards 1 inch burgundy wire edge ribbon

2 yards 1 inch deep moss green wire edge ribbon

1 8 inch clay flower pot

1 8 inch block Styrofoam™

Handful florist moss

2 yards 1 1/2 inch forest green and gold wire edge ribbon

Craft paint—fern green, burgundy and cream

Natural sea sponge

Glue gun/glue sticks

 Mix each craft paint color with almost an equal amount of water and sponge colors onto flowerpot. Allow paint to dry thoroughly.

 Tie cranberry and moss ribbons into two loop bows without streamers and glue bows to tree, distributing colors evenly.

 Tie green and gold ribbon in a large six loop bow to front of flowerpot. Drape streamers around to back of pot and secure with glue.

 Trim and glue Styrofoam™ block into flowerpot. Anchor topiary shape into pot and place moss around base of tree.

 Glue pine sprigs, dried roses, flowers and berries to cover tree shapes. Take care that colors are distributed evenly. Glue tiny sprigs of gypsophila to topiary.

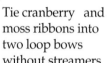

ENGLISH SCONE RECIPE

2 cups self-rising flour
1 Tablespoon baking powder
Pinch salt
1 to 1 1/3 cup cold milk
4 Tablespoons cold butter
1/2 cup currants

Preheat oven to 425. Blend flour, baking powder, salt and currants. Rub cold butter into mix with your fingers. Add milk and stir. Place dough on a well floured cloth and roll to about 1/2 inch thickness. Cut rounds with a cutter. Place scones on buttered, floured baking sheet and bake 8 to 10 minutes.

TEDDY'S CHRISTMAS

Bears need Christmas too...Create a sweet teddy bear's Christmas scene for the hearth or table display.

MATERIALS FOR TEDDY'S FURNITURE

1 small table and chair set

Acrylic craft paint—medium green and deep red

Red and green waterproof marking pens

Natural sea sponge

MATERIALS FOR TEDDY'S TOPIARY

1 3 inch Styrofoam™ ball

Handful small dried leaves

36 tiny red berries

Twig for tree trunk

Tiny amount of moss

1 small flowerpot (this pot is a napkin ring found in a variety store)

Glue gun/glue sticks

MATERIALS FOR TEDDY'S TREE

1 3 foot artificial tree

Small pine cones— approximately 50

30 small red tassels

Small dried flowers

Red embroidery floss

30 small green berries

1 gold applique star

Glue gun/glue sticks

 Paint table and chairs green; two coats will give perfect coverage on raw wood.

 Simply fill the little pot with oasis and press twigs in place. Place moss around tree base. Press twigs into Styrofoam™ ball and proceed to glue leaves onto ball, until surface is covered. Glue berries to topiary.

1 Tie 20 small bunches of dried flowers with red floss bows. Glue cones, tassels, berries and tiny bouquets to tree. Take care to place items evenly. Glue gold star to tree top.

 Mix red paint with an equal amount of water and lightly sponge edges of table and chairs. Allow paint to dry completely.

TINY PRESENTS
Cut small blocks of florist's oasis or Styrofoam™ and wrap tiny presents in scraps of cloth, ribbon or papers. Tiny bows and decorations, complete these little gifts.

 Use marking pens to draw tiny berries and vines on table corners.

VICTORIAN ANGEL

Crown the tree with the sweetest of angels. Dressed in the colors of Christmas, she presides over festivities and blesses this special time...

MATERIALS FOR ANGEL

1 China doll head with soft hair

1 8 inch heavy cardboard tube

1/2 yard deep green iridescent fabric

6 cotton balls or small amount batting

3 yards 3/4 inch burgundy wire edge ribbon

12 inches 1/2 inch burgundy gross gain ribbon

8 inches scalloped trim

8 inches cream ribbon rose trim

5 inches 1/2 inch gold wire edge ribbon

1 8 inch Battenburg lace doily

3 small dried roses

3 stems tiny red berries

Small sprigs preserved gypsophila

Small sprigs tiny white blossoms

Florist wire—heavy gage

Glue gun/glue sticks

1 Glue florist wire to inside of doll's head. Thread wire through cardboard tube and secure wire end. Place tube in a stable position for dressing doll. I used a dowel anchored in Styrofoam™.

2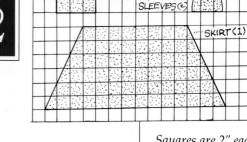

Cut fabric shapes as shown.

Squares are 2" each

3

Glue back seam of skirt and sleeves on wrong-side and turn to right-side. Stuff sleeves with cotton balls or batting.

4

Glue bodice, sleeves and skirt to cardboard tube.

5 Tie a small loop bow of wire edge ribbon, allowing two streamers to measure 16 inches. Cut two additional streamers of 18 inch length and add to bow. Glue bow as a bustle to back of dress.

6

Pinch and wire center of lace doily to form wings. Glue wings to angel's back.

7

Glue ribbon roses around angel's head and glue gold ribbon to form a halo attached to back of her head.

8 Glue scalloped pearl trim around bodice of dress. Finally, arrange a small bouquet of dried flowers and roses. Tie with gross grain ribbon and glue flowers to angel where her hands would be.

SCARLET TREE SKIRT

Satin roses and long scarlet silk tassels dress the tree. Rich Victorian textures and color create the backdrop for gaily decorated packages...

MATERIALS

1 1/2 yards 54 wide red moire fabric

4 yards 3/4 inch red satin cord

11 large red ribbon roses

11 4 inch red silk tassels

2 1/2 yards burgundy silk cord

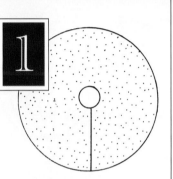

1 Cut one 48 inch circle of red moire ribbon. Fold circle to find center and cut a six inch circle in center. Cut through from center to circle's edge. Hem all edges.

2 Glue large cord around hem at edge of fabric.

3 Using 12 inches burgundy cord, one tassel and one ribbon rose, form rose medallion and glue to skirt as shown.

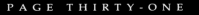

VICTORIAN GLASS ORNAMENTS

Silk fringe, ribbons and trim give ordinary glass balls a true Victorian flair. Easy to make, these holiday ornaments are wonderful gifts.

Materials given are for glass ornaments measuring 7 1/2 inch circumference.

MATERIALS FOR ORNAMENT A

1 gold glass ball

3 inches 3 inch white fringe

8 inches 1/2 inch white gimp

20 inches small gold beads

9 large pearls

9 inches gold wire edge ribbon

1 small cream silk rose

6 inches fine craft wire

Glue gun/glue sticks

1
Glue top of fringe around metal ornament cap. Gather fringe ends at bottom of ornament and wire to create tassel.

2
Glue white gimp around circumference of ornament. This will further secure fringe strands.

3
Glue bead strands around ornament at both top and bottom edges of gimp. Glue bead strands around tassel top.

4
Glue single, large pearls at 1/2 inch intervals on gimp center.

5
Form three ribbon loops and glue to front of ornament top.

6
Glue silk rose to front of bow sections.

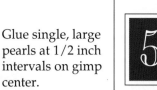

Ornaments B and C use same measurements of alternate trims and colors. Fringe is available in many colors, usually in the home decorating section of fabric stores. These are just three examples of the same technique.

ORNAMENT B

ORNAMENT A

ORNAMENT C

POTPOURRI AND ROSES ORNAMENT

Clear glass baubles filled with potpourri blend texture and scent...perfect treasures to give or keep.

MATERIALS

1 clear glass ornament—approximately 7 inches in circumference

8 inches 1/2 inch ecru lace

16 inches pearl trim

1/2 yard 1 inch lace with pearled center

2 small dried roses with leaves

Handful rose potpourri—any potpourri may be substituted

Glue gun/glue stick

1 Carefully remove metal ornament cap and fill glass ball with potpourri. Place metal cap on ornament.

2 Glue lace around center portion of glass.

3 Glue pearl trim to both top and bottom edges of lace.

4 Tie a four loop bow of pearly centered lace and glue to front of metal cap.

5 Glue one rose to bow center and one rose to lace as shown. Glue leaves to soften rose shape.

Try filling clear glass balls with cloves, tiny berries or pearls. Ribbons and laces can be coordinated to your color scheme.

ROSE SCENTED ANGELS

December brings fresh fallen snow...cheerful candles light the winter nights and tell of the arrival of Christmas. Sweetly scented angels are ready to delight family and friends...

ROSE SCENTED ANGELS MATERIALS

1 7 1/2 inch circle of lace

1 3/4 inch wooden bead

Small amount fine, soft yarn—any natural hair color will work beautifully

8 inches 1/4 inch red or green ribbon

2 inches tiny pearly trim

1 small silk ribbon rose

9 inches 1/2 inch fluted pearl gimp

6 small jewels, red or green

1 small piece paper lace ribbon or paper doily

9 inches gold cord

Fine tip markers: pink & black

4 inches fine wire

Handful rose potpourri—any scent may be substituted

Glue gun/glue sticks

1

Place potpourri in center of lace circle, gather lace edges and secure with wire.

2

Glue bead to center of lace ruff and glue on yarn to form angel's hair.

3

Glue pearl gimp around angel's skirt.

4

Glue jewels to lace ruff or down angel's dress for "buttons". Glue ribbon rose just below face.

5

Glue pearl trim to form halo. Glue cord to angel's back to form hanger. Secure hanger with a dot of glue to back of head to allow angel to hang straight.

6

Cut out small rounded wing shapes from paper lace ribbon or doily and glue to back. Use marker pens to make two black dots for eyes and pink marker for cheek dots. Three tiny pink dots will create a sweet mouth.

Angels in Velvet can be made using the steps above. Simply substitute a red velvet circle for the lace and add an apron of crocheted lace. Small Battenburg lace doilies gathered in the center make beautiful wings.

WREATHS FOR THE TREE
&
LITTLE CHRISTMAS BIRDS

Tiny wreaths, so simple to decorate with scraps of ribbon and dried materials are a wonderful Christmas project for children. Make wreaths for small birds with just the smallest amount of dried leaves and berries.

WREATH MATERIALS

1 2 inch twig wreath

24 inch lengths of ribbons or trim

Small amounts of dried leaves, berries, beads or tiny bells

8 inch section 1/8 ribbon for hanging loop

Glue gun/glue sticks

Glue ribbon end to wreath back as shown and twist ribbon around wreath, securing with glue dots.

 Glue small bows, trims and berries to wreath top. Decorations can be added to wreath bottom or sides for slightly different looks.

Glue 1/8 inch ribbon to wreath top, forming a loop for hanging.

LITTLE CHRISTMAS BIRD MATERIALS

1 2 1/2 inch bird

Small amount dried leaves and berries

3 inches red string or ribbon

Glue gun/Glue sticks

 Simply glue tiny leaves and berries around neck of bird to form a delicate wreath. Tie small bow of string or ribbon and glue in place.

GIFT IDEAS
Small wreaths make wonderful Christmas pins for jackets and sweaters. Simply glue a pin back to wreath. Use small wreaths as package decorations or on the front door of a doll house.

ELEGANT HOLIDAY ORNAMENTS

Ornate keepsakes grace the tree, scents of pine and cinnamon fill the air. Christmas has truly come...

Materials for ornament shown in center of next page.

MATERIALS

1 10 inch styrofoam™ ball

12 inches each—3/8 inch deep red gross grain ribbon, 1/4 inch red and gold braid trim

1 yard pearl trim

1 piece green velvet 12 by 12 inches

1/2 yard 1 inch deep red wire edge ribbon

9 inches gold cord

3 small textured gold beads

1 3/4 inch oblong gold bead

1 large fluted gold bead

1 large filigree gold drop bead

1 3 inch gold bead wire

Glue gun/glue sticks

1

Glue green velvet to styrofoam™ ball as shown. Trim away excess velvet.

2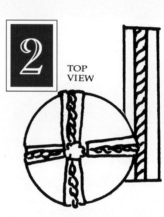

TOP VIEW

Glue red and gold braid to center of gross grain ribbon and glue to ornament as shown.

3

Glue pearls to ornament as shown.

4

Thread beads on bead wire and insert into bottom of ornament. Glue pearls around top gold bead to secure.

5

Tie a six loop bow of wire edge ribbon and glue to top of ornament. Puff bow to form a ruff encircling ornament top. This bow will hide any raw edges of glued velvet.

6 Glue gold braid to bow center to form hanging loop.

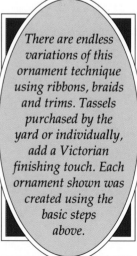

There are endless variations of this ornament technique using ribbons, braids and trims. Tassels purchased by the yard or individually, add a Victorian finishing touch. Each ornament shown was created using the basic steps above.

VICTORIAN TUSSIE-MUSSIES & VICTORIAN PAPER LACE CONES

Dressed in nosegays of scarlet roses, frilled in lace and pristine paper cones filled with treats...a Christmas tree for the romantic.

Tussie-Mussies were given during Victorian times as tokens of affection. The classic Tussie-Mussie has a rose in the center, surrounded by small flowers, greens and lace. Red rosebuds signify the pure and lovely.

MATERIALS FOR TUSSIE-MUSSIES

1 small red silk rosebud

1 small spray preserved gypsophila

1 small spray dried red blossoms

1 3 inch white paper doily

Florist tape

VICTORIAN PAPER LACE CONES MATERIALS

1 8 inch oval paper lace doily

6 inches 1/2 inch gold and red braid or trim

1/2 yard 1/4 inch Christmas green ribbon with picot edge

5 small red berry bunches

6 small green silk leaves

1 piece green construction paper for lining (optional)

Glue gun/glue sticks

1 Cut rosebud stem wire to two inch length and tape small flowers around rose bud with florist tape. Use a pulling, rolling motion while taping.

2 Puncture center of paper doily with taped wire and gently pull nosegay through hole until flowers are framed in lace. Ruffled lace fabric may be substituted for paper doily, but must be glued in place.

GIFT IDEA

Victorian paper cones can be filled with wrapped sweets, potpourri or tiny gifts.

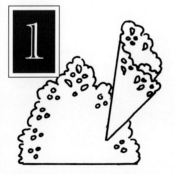

1 Cut paper doily in half and fold to create cone as shown. Glue back seam to secure. Insert a small piece of green construction paper for stiffness and to allow green color to show through lace pattern (lining is optional).

2 Glue gold trim around top of cone shape 1/2 inch from paper edge.

3 Tie a small bow and glue to cone as pictured. Glue a 7 inch ribbon section to cone for hanger. Glue berries and leaves to bow and top of hanger.

VELVET AND JEWEL HEARTS

Hearts of gold, hearts of velvet...Symbols of love decorate the tree, make beautiful presents, and can even be used as window shade pulls.

VELVET AND JEWEL HEARTS MATERIALS

2 heart shapes of light cardboard or heavy paper cut to pattern shape

2 4 inch by 4 inch pieces of velvet or moire fabric

2 heart shapes light batting cut to pattern shape

12 inches braid or pearls

1 gold metal filigree shape—these are earring shapes found in your craft store

Jewels, pearls, gold beads—four to six per ornament

1 small silk tassel—purchased by the yard

1 9 inch piece gold cord for hanging loop

Tracing paper and pencil

Glue gun/glue sticks

1 Trace heart, and cut out shape. Use cut out pattern to cut two hearts of light cardboard or heavy paper.

4 Glue fabric to cardboard hearts as shown.

7 Glue gold filigree piece to heart center. Glue beads or jewels to filigree piece. Glue tassel to heart bottom.

2 Lay traced heart shape on wrong-side of fabrics and draw around shape with a 1/4 inch seam allowance as shown. Cut two fabric hearts.

5 Glue hearts together as shown.

8 Glue 9 inch gold cord piece to top of heart to form a loop for hanging ornament.

3 Glue cotton batting to one side of each heart shape. Trim away excess batting.

6 Glue braid or beads around edge of heart.

GOLD HEARTS
These gold heart ornaments are purchased at your craft store and are simply decorated by gluing trims around the edges. Filigree shapes were glued to heart center and decorated with jewels. A tassel and hanging loop were glued in place.

Heart Pattern

BELLS OF CHRISTMAS & BASKETS FOR THE TREE

Joyful music fills the winter air...the bells of Christmas ring in the blessed season, and lovely little baskets adorned with ribbons and berries grace the tree.

BELLS MATERIALS

1 1 1/2 inch diameter brass bell

6 tiny brass bells

15 inches 1/4 scarlet ribbon

5 inches 1/2 inch hunter green silk ribbon

1 sprig preserved gypsophila

6 small red berry bunches

5 small white berry bunches

1 small sprig dried green flowers

Glue gun/glue sticks

1 Thread hunter green ribbon through top bell slot and tie or glue to secure. Knot will be covered by berries and flowers.

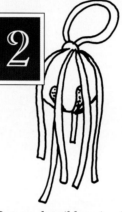

2 Cut scarlet ribbon in six equal lengths and glue to bell top as shown.

3 Tie one small bell to each ribbon end, sliding each bell to a slightly different placement on ribbon before tying. Trim ribbon ends.

4 Glue berries, gypsophila and dried flowers to bell top, creating a small floral pouf.

BASKETS MATERIALS

1 3 inch red basket

8 inches 1/4 inch printed ribbon (this print was trimmed from a wider ribbon)

Small amount dried leaves

7 bunches tiny red berries

1 small red silk ribbon rose

Glue gun/glue sticks

1 Twist ribbon around basket handle, securing ribbon ends with glue. Tie small bow and glue to handle top.

2 Glue sprigs of leaves and berries to basket edge to form a delicate wreath effect.

3 Glue one silk ribbon rose to bow center.

BELLS OF CHRISTMAS

BASKETS FOR THE TREE

GARNET AND GOLD WREATH

Snow brushes the window panes, friends gather to share Christmas cheer and they can hardly believe you've made this exquisite wreath yourself. Garnet red, glittering gold and deep pine green combine to create a perfect holiday color formula.

MATERIALS

1 22 inch artificial pine wreath

5 flat, gold Christmas ornaments with music motif

4 medium pine cones sprayed gold

3 packs gold craft charms—15 charms in all

12 gold fleur de lis shaped buttons

5 large gold filigree earring findings

2 1 inch gold heart shapes

5 large fluted gold beads

2 bunches gold and glittered dried gypsophila

3 yards 1 1/2 inch garnet red wire-edged ribbon with gold fleur de lis pattern

Glue gun/glue sticks

1 Glue ornaments, charms, cones, buttons, hearts, earring findings and beads onto wreath in a scattered pattern. Distribute the small decorations evenly.

2 Tie a large six loop bow with loops measuring approximately three inches each. Glue bow to upper left side of wreath as pictured. Twirl streamers to encircle wreath and tack in place with dots of glue.

3 Glue small sprigs of glittery gold gypsophila into wreath among ornaments and ribbon.

Gypsohila (Baby's Breath) can be sprayed with gold spray paint and sprinkled with gold glitter in the event that it cannot be found in your craft store. Ornaments as well, can be sprayed with gold paint.

TAPESTRY AND LACE WREATH
&
VICTORIAN HALO WREATH

T'was the night before Christmas and all through the house...festive Victorian wreaths wait to surprise and delight Father Christmas. Perhaps he will linger a bit longer and leave a few more special presents!

TAPESTRY AND LACE WREATH MATERIALS

1 16 inch straw wreath

2 1/2 yards each: pink and blue wire edged tapestry ribbon

5 yards 4 inch wide ecru ruffled lace

3 sprays Christmas berries with leaves

2 1/2 yards wired gold beads

2 1/2 yards small pearl trim

1 bunch white gypsophila

Florist wire

Glue gun/glue sticks

VICTORIAN HALO WREATH MATERIALS

1 6 inch grapevine wreath

2 1/2 yards 1 1/2 inch paper lace

1 yard 1/2 inch iridescent pink non-woven ribbon

4 sprays small beige silk roses with leaves

1 spray white gypsophila

Glue gun/glue sticks

1 Glue ruffled lace around outer and inner edges of wreath form.

4 Separate berries from main stem and glue berries with leaves throughout wreath.

1 Cut both ribbons into three inch lengths and form individual loops. Glue loops to wreath, mixing paper and pink ribbons evenly.

2 Using both tapestry ribbons, form bows with two loops each as shown. Secure bow centers with florist wire and glue bows to cover wreath as shown.

5 Glue pearls and gold beads to wreath. Use swirling shapes and secure to ribbons to hold swirl shapes.

2 Remove roses and leaves from main stems. Glue roses and leaves into ribbon loops.

3 Glue remaining lace to wreath, in between bows for a full shape.

6 Glue sprigs of gypsophila among ribbons and lace.

3 Glue tiny sprigs of white flowers among ribbons and roses.

The technique used to create both wreaths is essentially the same. Loops of lace and ribbon are glued to the wreath form. Flowers, berries and beads are added for accents and color. Experiment with all styles of lace for different effects.

TAPESTRY AND LACE WREATH

VICTORIAN
HALO WREATH

SUGAR PLUM WREATH

Scent woven with texture and shape...create the message of Christmas love so easily! Plum potpourri adds a spicy fragrance to the room and delights the eye.

MATERIALS

1 large bag plum scented potpourri—any holiday potpourri may be substituted.

1 12 inch heart shaped straw wreath

1 bunch plum/pink preserved gypsophila

1 yard 3/4 inch deep red gross grain ribbon

Glue gun/glue sticks

1 Pour potpourri into a large ceramic or glass bowl and proceed to glue individual potpourri pieces to wreath. Cover front and sides of wreath well.

2 Glue small sprigs of gypsophila to wreath, scattering the sprigs evenly.

3 Tie a four loop bow and glue to upper left section of wreath. Twirl ribbon streamers and secure twirls and ribbon ends to wreath with glue.

Potpourri placed in bowls to scent the room have only the top layer of dried materials exposed to air. This wreath exposes all of the perfume at once and when hung gives much more scent to a room.

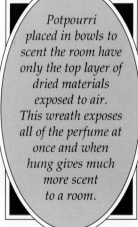

WREATH OF MEMORIES

My favorite wreath of all...this one is filled with special little mementos. Each Wreath of Memories will be unique! Collect small treasures from shelves and hidden away boxes to display on a wreath of your very own. Of all the wreaths I have ever made, this one always gets the most compliments.

MATERIALS

1 30 inch artificial pine wreath

60 small mementos

20 small 4 loop bows—each ribbon is different

4 yards red wired beads

Glue gun/glue sticks

 1 Simply glue your little treasures to the wreath, scattering the colors and items evenly.

 2 Tie ribbon scraps of all kinds into bows and glue bows to the wreath. Colors will mix well, the wreath shown includes plaids, patterns, purples and pinks, as well as traditional reds and greens. Lace can be tied in small bows and added.

 3 Glue red wired beads to wreath in a twining pattern. Tack beads to wreath with dots of glue.

SUGGESTIONS FOR DECORATING A WREATH OF MEMORIES

Tiny framed photos, Small teddy bears, Ornaments, Shells, Tiny sachet bags, Bells, Dried roses, Little birds, Single earrings, Small wooden animals, Christmas stickers, Lucky pennies, Painted eggs, Gold lockets, Small china figures, Berries, Little baskets, Tiny wrapped boxes.

Create a Wreath of Memories for grandmother using little framed photos and small craft items the children have made. She can display it all year long.

WINTER HERB WREATH
&
SEASON'S CHEER WREATH

Herald in the season of Christmas with a wreath for every room of the house. Delicate herbs and flowers grace a bedroom wall. Scented eucalyptus and berries decorate the entry hall, greeting chilled visitors to the warmth of your home.

WINTER HERB WREATH MATERIALS

1 12 inch straw wreath

1 large bunch preserved gypsophila

2 bunches dried white flowers

1 bunch red celosia—a feathery plumed annual flower (or a dried substitute in the same color range)

2 bunches dried ornamental oregano or substitute

Glue gun/glue sticks

1 Glue a ruff (a frilled or pleated pattern) of preserved gypsophila around outer edge of wreath. Glue a smaller ruff around inner edge.

2 Glue oregano and celosia to front of wreath, working pieces in as shown.

SEASON'S CHEER WREATH MATERIALS

1 14 inch eucalyptus wreath

4 sprays small cream colored fruits

4 sprays small black berries

1 bunch pepper berries

1 spray preserved gypsophila

7 small pine cones

2 yards each; 1 1/2 inch teal moire ribbon, 34 inch green and burgundy plaid ribbon

Glue gun/glue sticks

 1 Glue berries and fruit to wreath. Space berries and fruit evenly.

 2 Glue sprigs of gypsophila among berries and fruits.

 3 Glue plaid ribbon down the center of moire ribbon to create a striped effect. Trim a three inch section from one end. Tie long ribbon into a four loop bow. Secure bow center with florist wire. Glue a three inch section around bow center and glue finished bow to wreath as pictured.

WINTER HERB WREATH

SEASON'S CHEER
WREATH

CHRISTMAS ROSE WREATH

Rose scent mingles deliciously with cedar, candles are alight and a favorite Christmas book waits to be read once again. Create a beautiful wreath to perfume the winter air.

MATERIALS

1 26 inch green cedar wreath

10 white silk roses

13 red silk roses—these are "dried" looking silk...standard silk roses may be substituted

1 bunch dried white larkspur

1 bunch dried white gypsophila

2 yards each: 2 3/4 inch cream moire ribbon with fleur de lis pattern, 1 inch hunter green satin ribbon

1/2 inch rose red gross grain ribbon

5 inch piece florist wire

Glue gun/glue sticks

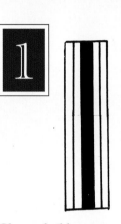

Glue red ribbon to center portion of hunter green ribbon. Glue the striped green and red ribbon to center of cream ribbon to create a long three-colored ribbon.

Tie a large four loop bow and secure center with wire. Trim two inches from one streamer to use for bow center. Glue as shown. Glue or wire bow to upper right section of wreath.

Glue roses, dried larkspur and gypsophila into wreath in a scattered pattern. Distribute flowers in a fairly even fashion.

Roses may be scented with essential oil before adding to wreath. Simply touch base or back of roses lightly, scent can be restored occasionally with addition of rose oil.

ENGLISH HOLIDAY WREATH

Memories of Christmas's in England...with hearth fires blazing and the family all together. Snow covers the slate rooftops and this cheery little wreath decorates a dining room wall.

MATERIALS

1 12 inch straw wreath

10 sprays green silk leaves of mixed shapes and greens. (Leaves used were actually all leftovers from projects which used only the flowers.)

1 small brass horn ornament

3 yards wired gold beads

6 yards 1 1/2 inch wire edged red ribbon with gold detail

1 2 1/2 inch brass bell

1 yard gold cord

1 bunch dried white tea flowers or small blossoms

Florist wire

Glue gun/Glue sticks

1 Glue green leaves to cover wreath form.

4 Glue sprigs of dried tea flowers to wreath just behind each bow to form sprays. Glue red berries to dried flowers.

2 Tie four six loop bows, securing bow center with florist wire. Each bow will take a 44 inch length of ribbon. Glue bows to wreath as pictured and cut remaining ribbon in three sections. Glue these streamers to bottom bow and trim each streamer to a slightly different length.

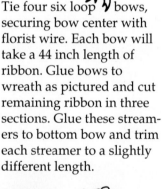

Cut four eight inch lengths of wired beads and four five inch lengths of wired beads. Glue coiled end to wreath just under bottom bow and gently pull coil downward to create a curled streamer of beads.

3 Glue brass horn to left of bottom bow.

6 Cut gold cord in three sections. Tie brass bell to one section and glue all three cords to wreath, just below bottom bow. Trim two plain cords to slightly different lengths and knot cord ends.

CHRISTMAS VELVET WREATH

Rich, deep colors all tied in a lush maroon red velvet bow make this wreath perfect for the door or study. Collect pine cones all year round to add thoughts of special walks to your Christmas wreath.

MATERIALS

1 18 inch straw wreath

52 medium size pine cones—cones of all kinds can be mixed for this wreath

12 picks—snow flecked artificial pine

14 small deep red artificial apples

6 bunches artificial grapes

3 stems artificial acorns

2 stems shiny deep red berries

2 yards 1 1/2 inch deep maroon red wire edged ribbon

Glue gun/glue sticks

1

Glue pine cones in an evenly spaced pattern on wreath.

4

Form a large six loop bow of velvet ribbon. Secure bow center with wire and glue a three inch loop of ribbon to create bow center as shown. Glue bow to wreath as pictured.

2 Separate sections of artifical pine and glue singular pieces to wreath among pine cones.

3 Glue apples, berries, grapes and acorns to wreath, filling in any gaps between cones and pine.

BATTENBURG LACE BASKET
&
CHRISTMAS SACHETS

Thoughtful gifts are so easy to create. Christmas potpourri fills little sachets of berry red and green, all trimmed with lace and embroideries.

MATERIALS FOR BASKET

1 small oval basket

1 square Battenburg lace doily

14 inches white lace trim

12 inches 1 inch deep red gross grain ribbon

3 small dried roses with leaves

Tiny sprig preserved gypsophila

Glue gun/glue sticks

MATERIALS FOR SACHET BAGS

3 inch by 5 inch pieces of moire, silk or velvet in Christmas colors

Gold braids and trims

Gold cordings

*Hand or machine stitch

 Cut center from doily and glue lace trim over basket edges. Glue white lace to inside of basket over cut doily edges to create a finished effect.

 Tie a four loop bow of red ribbon and glue to basket. Glue roses, leaves and gypsophila to bow center.

 Stitch two 3 by 5 inch rectangles together to create a small pouch.

 Hem top seam and turn fabric right-side out. Glue or stitch gold braids or trim around top edge of pouch and fill with potpourri. Tie sachet with a bit of gold cord.

SACHET ENVELOPE
Simply glue one 7 inch by 4 inch cloth rectangle as shown. Glue trim over edges or ribbon rose.

GIFTS FROM THE KITCHEN

Taking time during the holidays to make tasty gifts is one of the most delightful traditions of Christmas. Decorate a small basket of treats for the perfect hostess gift.

MATERIALS FOR BASKET

1 10 inch basket

1 green and white woven kitchen cloth

5 sprays fresh pine

18 small red berries, wired in groups of three

24 small pine cones

Glue guns/glue sticks

 Cut one 30 inch by 1 inch strip from kitchen cloth. If fabric is not long enough, simply piece two strips together at handle—bow will cover fabric ends. Fold and iron 1/4 inch along each side of strip to create a finished edge. Glue fold to secure. Glue strip around top edge of basket.

 Cut two 12 inch by 3 inch strips of cloth. Fold and iron edges under 1/2 inches along each strip side and glue fold in place. Glue strip ends together and pinch center to create a cloth bow. Glue a small strip of folded fabric around center to create bow center. Repeat for second bow and glue a bow to each side of basket, just below handle.

 Glue pine sprays, berries and cones to basket front and handle.

APPLE CHUTNEY

4 Pounds peeled sour apples
1 Pound raisins
1/2 Pound chopped onions
1 Tablespoon mustard seed, crushed
1 Tablespoon pickling spice
1 Teaspoon ground ginger
1 Lemon, grated rind and juice
1 1/2 Pint vinegar
2 Pounds brown sugar

Mince apples, onions and raisins. Add spices and mustard seed. Dissolve sugar in 1/2 pint vinegar and set aside. Add fruit mixture to remaining pint of vinegar until soft. Add sugar/vinegar mixture with lemon juice and rind. Cook until thickened. Pour into sterilized jars as you would jam.

LEMON CURD

8 oz. sugar
3 oz. butter
Grated rind and juice of three lemons
3 Eggs

Put sugar, butter and lemon in top of a double boiler to melt butter and blend. Whisk eggs and stir into lemon mixture. Stir constantly until mixture thickens—10 to 15 minutes. Do not let mixture boil. Place in jars and refrigerate.

SCENTED TEA CUSHIONS

The delicious aroma of potpourri escapes every time a mug of warm tea or coffee is placed on these lovely cushions of scent. Make several sets for gifts and one to keep. Friends will really love and appreciate a useful gift.

MATERIALS

1/4 yard Christmas print cotton

1/4 yard light reinforcement batting

2 yards 1/4 inch red cord

Fabric Glue

Potpourri—small pieces only. Wood chips will not work well for this project.

*Hand stitch or sewing machine

Note: Cushions can be constructed with fabric glue or with the use of a glue gun.

1 Cut two 5 inch squares of cloth for each mug cushion and two 7 1/2 squares for the teapot cushion. Sew or glue squares together, leaving one side open for filling.

2 Place a thin layer of batting, cut to size in each little cushion. Sprinkle about one handful of strongly scented potpourri. Large pieces of dried materials will not work well. I put potpourri through the blender to create a finer texture.

3 Stitch or glue opening shut. Glue cord around edges of cushions.

Scented cushions cannot be laundered, but fabric can be wiped with a damp cloth. Scented cushions stored in linen drawers will perfume kitchen linens beautifully.

CINNAMON KITCHEN ARRANGEMENT
&
WINTER ROSE WALL SACHETS

Simmering spiced cider and special ginger cookies...cinnamon all tied in scarlet ribbon...snow lightly falling...what joy to share time in the Christmas kitchen.

MATERIALS

1 bunch long cinnamon sticks

21 small red berries, wired in groups of three

7 silk holly leaves

1 bunch preserved gypsophila

1 spray dried German statice

5 small brass bells

1 yard 1 1/2 inch scarlet ribbon with gold edge

Florist wire

Glue gun/glue sticks

 Twist wire around center of cinnamon sticks to secure. Glue leaves, dried flowers and berries to cinnamon to form a floral spray.

 Tie a large four loop bow of ribbon and glue to cinnamon as shown.

 Glue bells to cinnamon just below bow.

Small cinnamon sticks tied in ribbons make wonderful ornaments for the tree. Simply add a loop of thin ribbon to hang cinnamon on the tree.

WINTER ROSE WALL SACHET MATERIALS

1 10 inch round Battenburg lace doily

Fabric Stiffener

Cardboard cone covered with foil

14 red silk roses

3 sprays preserved cedar

1 large spray white gypsophila

1 1/2 cups Victorian Christmas Potpourri

1 yard 1/2 inch gold wire edge ribbon

Glue gun/glue sticks

 Fold doily to form a cone. Shape and glue front seam in place. Follow instructions on fabric stiffener and place stiffened lace over a cone of cardboar,d covered with foil until lace dries.

 Fill cone with potpourri and arrange roses, cedar and gypsophila in sachet. Tie a pretty bow and glue to front of sachet.

Victorian Christmas Potpourri Recipe

COMFORTS OF CHRISTMAS...GOOD FRIENDS ARRIVE TO
A WARM WELCOME OF LAVISHLY DECORATED ROOMS
FILLED WITH THE SCENTS OF CHRISTMAS...

Ingredients

4 oz. rose hips

1 oz. rosemary

1/2 oz. peppermint leaves

2 bay leaves, broken

3 oz. uva ursi leaves or
any dried, dark green
leaves

2 handfuls tiny pine
cones

2 oz. small dried cedar
sprigs

2 tablespoons powdered
orris root

10 drops bayberry oil

2 drops cedar oil